Backyard Bugs
& Creepy-Crawlies

Grasshoppers

Ava Podmorow

Explore other books at:
WWW.ENGAGEBOOKS.COM

VANCOUVER, B.C.

www.engagebooks.com

Grasshoppers: Level Pre-1
Backyard Bugs & Creepy Crawlies
Podmorow, Av 2004 –
Text © 2022 Engage Books
Design © 2022 Engage Books

Edited by: A.R. Roumanis
and Sarah Harvey

Text set in Epilogue

FIRST EDITION / FIRST PRINTING

LIBRARY AND ARCHIVES CANADA CATALOGUING IN PUBLICATION

Title: Grasshoppers / Ava Podmorow.
Names: Podmorow, Ava, author.
Description: Series statement: Backyard bugs & creepy-crawlies
Engaging readers: level pre-1, beginner.

Identifiers: Canadiana (print) 20220403430 | Canadiana (ebook) 20220403449
ISBN 978-1-77476-708-5 (hardcover)
ISBN 978-177476-709-2 (softcover)
ISBN 978-177476-710-8 (epub)
ISBN 978-177476-711-5 (pdf)

Subjects:
LCSH: Grasshoppers—Juvenile literature.

Classification: LCC QL508.A2 P63 2022 | DDC J595.7/26   DC23

This project has been made possible in part
by the Government of Canada.

Canada

Chirp! Chirp!
Did you hear that
grasshopper?

Grasshoppers live in dry grassy areas.

Grasshoppers are insects.

Antennae

Legs

They have six legs,
two antennae, and
two pairs of wings.

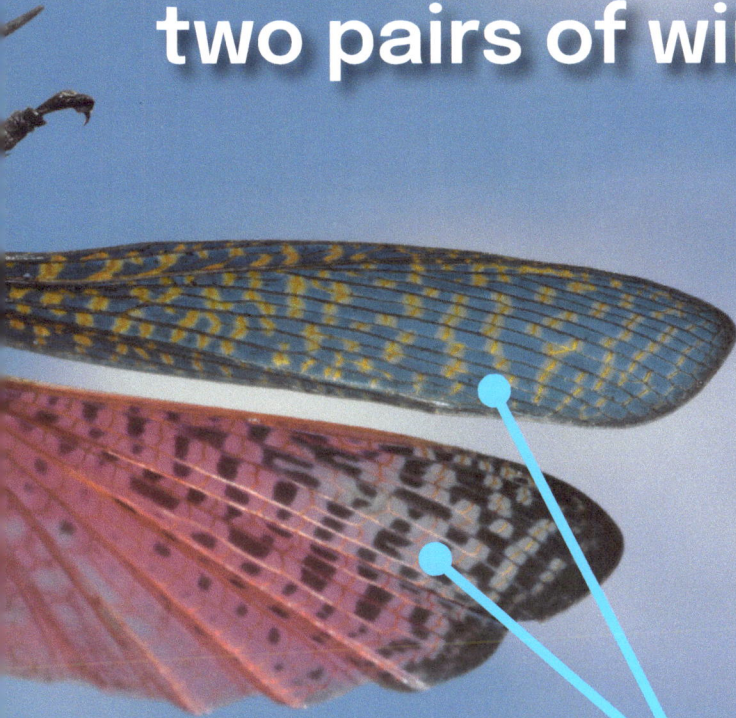

Wings

Grasshoppers use their antennae to touch and smell.

Grasshoppers feed on plants.

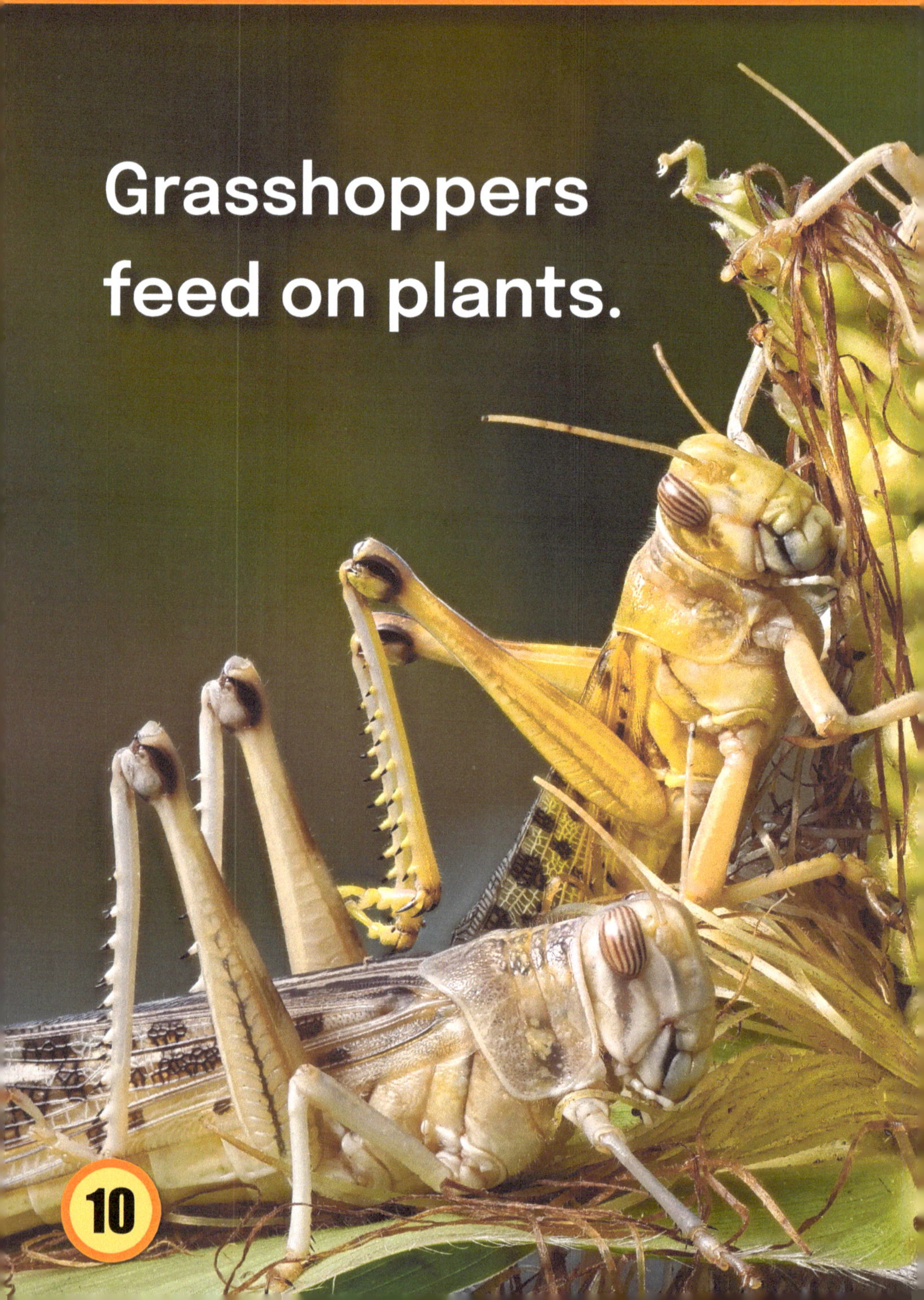

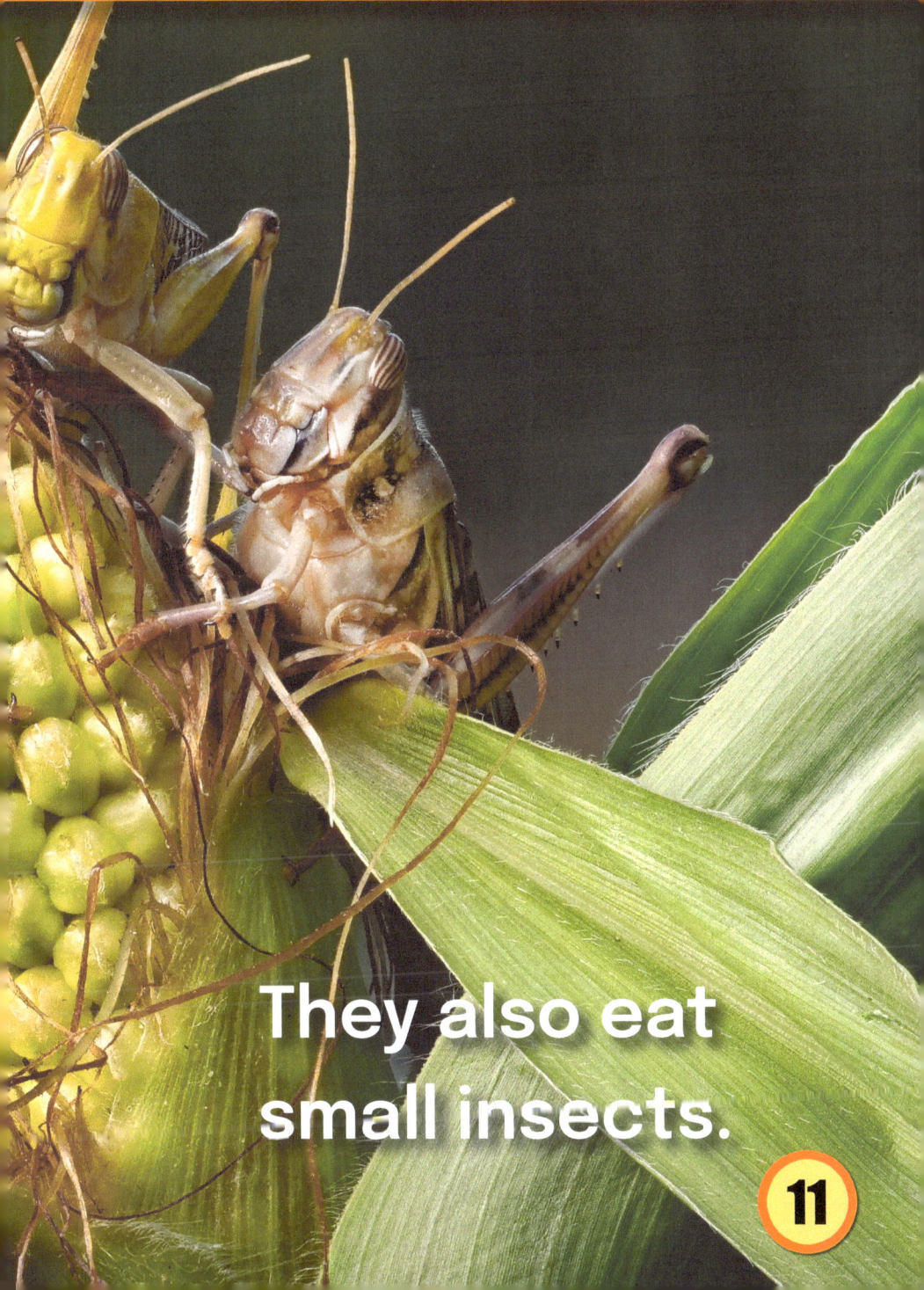

They also eat
small insects.

Mother grasshoppers bury their eggs in the soil.

Grasshoppers have close to one hundred babies in the summer and fall.

Grasshoppers feed on plants that may be harmful to Earth.

16

Hopping helps grasshoppers escape when they are in danger.

They are also
able to fly away.

Grasshoppers often hide when in danger.

They can look
like leaves.

21

Grasshoppers can jump really far.

Some grasshoppers can jump the length of a surfboard.

23

Grasshoppers make sounds by rubbing their wings together.

25

Some noises
grasshoppers make
sound like music!

Explore other books in the Backyard Bugs & Creepy Crawlies series!

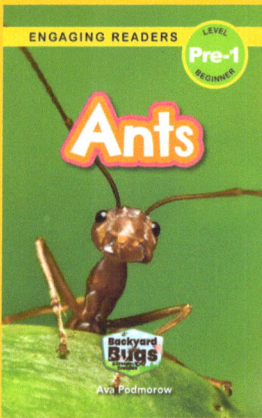

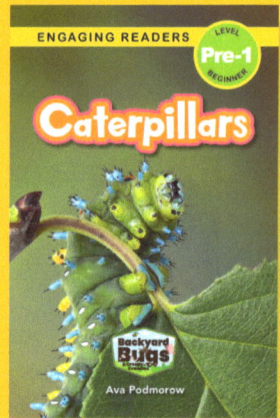

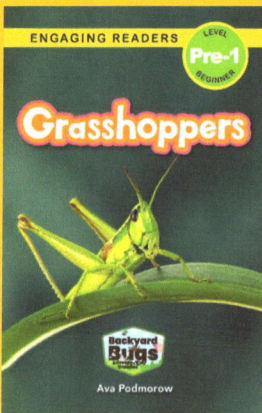

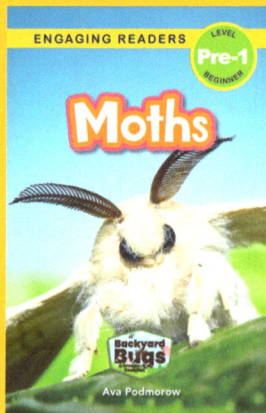

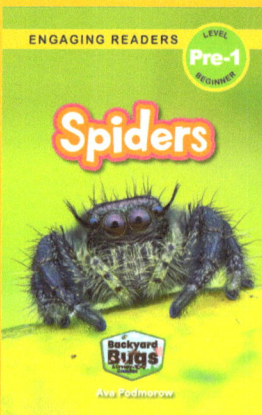

ENGAGING READERS — LEVEL Pre-1 BEGINNER
Ants
Backyard Bugs
Ava Podmorow

ENGAGING READERS — LEVEL Pre-1 BEGINNER
Beetles
Backyard Bugs
Victoria Hazlehurst

ENGAGING READERS — LEVEL Pre-1 BEGINNER
Caterpillars
Backyard Bugs
Ava Podmorow

ENGAGING READERS — LEVEL Pre-1 BEGINNER
Grasshoppers
Backyard Bugs
Ava Podmorow

ENGAGING READERS — LEVEL Pre-1 BEGINNER
Moths
Backyard Bugs
Ava Podmorow

ENGAGING READERS — LEVEL Pre-1 BEGINNER
Snails
Backyard Bugs
Ava Podmorow

ENGAGING READERS — LEVEL Pre-1 BEGINNER
Spiders
Backyard Bugs
Ava Podmorow

ENGAGING READERS — LEVEL Pre-1 BEGINNER
Wasps
Backyard Bugs
Sarah Harvey

ENGAGING READERS — LEVEL Pre-1 BEGINNER
Worms
Backyard Bugs
Victoria Hazlehurst

Explore books in the Animals In The City series.

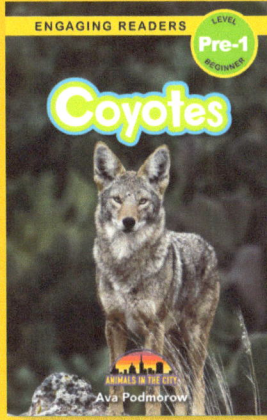

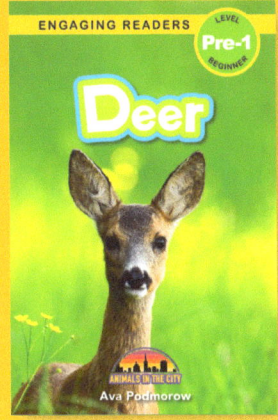

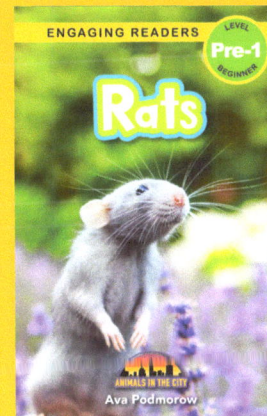

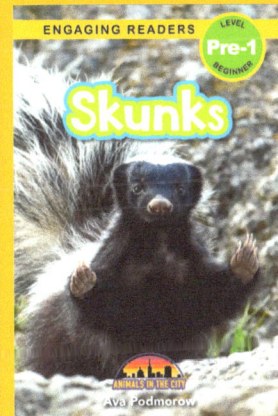

ENGAGING READERS — LEVEL Pre-1 BEGINNER — **Cats** — Ava Podmorow

ENGAGING READERS — LEVEL Pre-1 BEGINNER — **Coyotes** — Ava Podmorow

ENGAGING READERS — LEVEL Pre-1 BEGINNER — **Deer** — Ava Podmorow

ENGAGING READERS — LEVEL Pre-1 BEGINNER — **Owls** — Ava Podmorow

ENGAGING READERS — LEVEL Pre-1 BEGINNER — **Pigeons** — Ava Podmorow

ENGAGING READERS — LEVEL Pre-1 BEGINNER — **Rabbits** — Ava Podmorow

ENGAGING READERS — LEVEL Pre-1 BEGINNER — **Raccoons** — Sarah Harvey

ENGAGING READERS — LEVEL Pre-1 BEGINNER — **Rats** — Ava Podmorow

ENGAGING READERS — LEVEL Pre-1 BEGINNER — **Skunks** — Ava Podmorow

Visit www.engagebooks.com/readers

www.ingramcontent.com/pod-product-compliance
Lightning Source LLC
Chambersburg PA
CBHW040941100426
42813CB00017B/2894